TBD DEVASTATOR in action

By Al Adcock
Color by Don Greer
Illustrated by Perry Manley

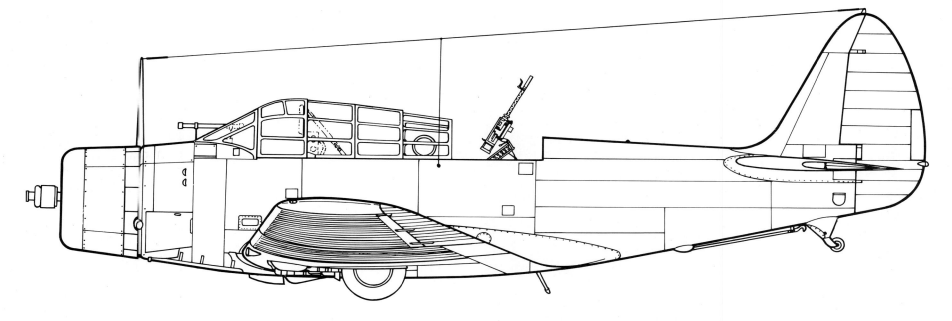

Aircraft Number 97
squadron/signal publications

A TBD-1 Devastator of Torpedo Squadron Two (VT-2) pulls away after making a torpedo attack on the Japanese Carrier SHOHO. TBDs of VT-2 and VT-3 are credited with sinking the SHOHO on 7 May 1942 during the Battle of the Coral Sea.

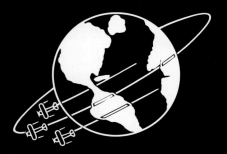

ISBN 0-89747-231-4

If you have any photographs of the aircraft, armor, soldiers or ships of any nation, particularly wartime snapshots, why not share them with us and help make Squadron/Signal's books all the more interesting and complete in the future. Any photograph sent to us will be copied and the original returned. The donor will be fully credited for any photos used. Please send them to:

Squadron/Signal Publications, Inc.
1115 Crowley Drive.
Carrollton, TX 75011-5010.

Dedication

To all the pilots and aircrewmen who flew the TBD Devastator and made the ultimate sacrifice so the United States would remain free.

Acknowledgements

I would like to thank the following people for their help with this project: Bill Larkins for sharing his extensive photo collection; Paul White of the National Archives for his help during my visit to Washington; Jim Presley, Joe Cason and Bill Johnson at the U.S. Naval Aviation Musuem; Harry Gann at McDonnell Douglas Aircraft for the many TBD photographs and drawings; CAPT William E. Scarborough for his invaluable help on the TBD-1A float plane; and Ann Millbroke at United Technologies Archives. Without their help this project would have been impossible.

Photo Credits

U.S. Navy	U.S. Naval Aviation Museum
Jim Presley	Smithsonian Institution
Will Taylor	San Diego Aero Space Museum
Joe Cason	National Air and Space Museum
Harry Gann	United Technologies Archives
John M. Elliott	CAPT William E. Scarborough USN (RET)
William T. Larkins	McDonnell Douglas Aircraft
National Archives	ADM Harlan T. Johnson USN (RET)
J.J. Frey	Naval Historical Center
Ray Wagner	Edo Corporation
Ralph Stell Jr.	CDR H.E. Hein USN (RET)
Susan Ewing	Charles E. Fosha
Jim Mesko	Walt Holmes

6-T-4, a TBD-1 (BuNo 0325) of Torpedo Squadron Six (VT-6) aboard USS ENTERPRISE makes a practice torpedo drop during training exercises held in October of 1941. (National Archives)

3

Introduction

During 1934, the U.S. Navy's aircraft carrier force was comprised of three carriers, USS LEXINGTON (CV-2), USS SARATOGA (CV-3), and USS RANGER (CV-4), with the air groups aboard these ships being equipped with biplane fighters, scouts, and torpedo bombers. During this time the Navy was beginning a massive expansion program and had four new aircraft carriers either under construction or on the drawing boards. These ships, USS YORKTOWN (CV-5), USS ENTERPRISE (CV-6), USS WASP (CV-7), and USS HORNET (CV-8), were all scheduled to be fully operational by 1941. To outfit the air groups aboard these new ships, the Navy sought proposals from the American aviation industry for new and improved aircraft.

In June of 1934, the Navy Bureau of Aeronautics (BuAer) issued a request for proposals to various aviation companies for design submissions for a new torpedo bomber to replace both the Martin BM-2 and Great Lakes TG-2 biplane torpedo bombers then in service with fleet torpedo (VT) squadrons. The specification called for an aircraft that could carry the Bliss-Leavitt Mk XIII aerial torpedo, or up to three 500 pound bombs, or a combination of 100 pound and 500 pound bombs. The specification also called for use of the 900 hp Pratt & Whitney XR-1830-60 air cooled radial engine. This engine had just completed its development tests and had been cleared for production.

Two companies, Great Lakes Aircraft of Cleveland, Ohio and Douglas Aircraft of Santa Monica, California, submitted proposals to the Bureau of Aeronautics for consideration and both were awarded prototype development contracts. The Great Lakes entry was designated the XTBG-1, while the Douglas entry received the designation XTBD-1. The Great Lakes XTBG-1 (BuNo 9723) was the last biplane torpedo bomber considered by the U.S. Navy. It had an all metal semi-monocoque fuselage, with fabric covered wings and tail surfaces. The bombardier was housed in the fuselage ahead of the pilot, under an abbreviated canopy, with the bomb aiming window being located under the fuselage between the main landing gear legs. Tests with the prototype revealed that the XTBG-1 had poor performance and unstable flight characteristics. Based on these test results, the Navy rejected the design. Great Lakes built one other experimental aircraft, the XB2G-1, before the company went out of business during 1936.

The Douglas Aircraft XTBD-1 prototype (BuNo 9720) differed considerably from the design drawings originally submitted by Douglas to the Navy. The original concept, known as the VT-VB Airplane at Douglas, closely resembled the Northrop BT-1; however, the design was changed before construction began on the prototype at the Douglas Santa Monica facility. The XTBD-1 emerged as an all metal, low-wing monoplane with a semi-monocoque fuselage and fabric covered control surfaces.

The prototype had a wing span of fifty feet, making it necessary to have the twelve foot outer wing panels fold upward for storage aboard ship. While most carrier based aircraft of this time had manually folded wings, the XTBD-1 featured hydraulic upward folding wings that, when fully folded, had the wing tips touching just over the canopy. To allow for a slower approach and landing speed, full span trailing edge flaps were installed on the inner wing panels.

The crew of three, pilot, assistant pilot/bombardier/torpedo aimer, and radioman/gunner, were housed in the fuselage under a long framed greenhouse type canopy. The radioman/gunner occupied the rearmost position and was provided with a single Colt-Browning .30 caliber M2 machine gun on a flexible ring mount with 600 rounds of ammunition. Provision was made for a second .30 caliber machine gun, with 500 rounds of ammunition, to be mounted in the starboard side of the cowling, synchronized to fire through the propeller arc. For gunnery practice, provision was made for mounting a gun camera externally on the starboard side of the cowling, just below the cockpit.

The main armament, the Mk XIII torpedo, was housed under the fuselage in a recessed mount. When mounted the forward portion of the torpedo extended down into the slipstream. While this was an improvement over earlier torpedo bombers which carried the torpedo fully exposed, the downward protruding torpedo warhead did cause considerable drag.

The main landing gear retracted rearward into shallow wells on the underside of the wing and when fully retracted, the wheels remained semi-exposed. This feature allowed the XTBD-1 to be landed on its belly with only minimal damage to the fuselage. Originally the tail wheel was retractable; however, this was later changed to a fixed tail wheel which was not retractable. The XTBD-1 was the first Navy aircraft to feature main landing gear wheel brakes, having Bendix aircraft brakes installed on each main landing gear wheel. For many years the Navy had shunned the use of aircraft brakes, thinking them unsafe and difficult to use aboard ship. The arresting hook was installed just in front of the tail wheel and lay flush against the underside of the fuselage when not in use.

The prototype weighed in at 5,270 pounds empty and had a maximum takeoff weight of 8,930 pounds (armed with a 2,000 pound torpedo). The XTBD-1 made its first flight on 15 April 1935 and was ferried to the Anacostia Naval Air Station at Washington, D.C. on 24 April to begin Navy acceptance testing. Acceptance trials were conducted over an eight month period during which the XTBD-1 was flown at the Naval Air Proving Ground at Dahlgren, Virginia and the Norfolk Experimental Naval Air Station at Norfolk, Virginia. Carrier suitability trials were held at NAS North Island, California and aboard USS LEXINGTON (CV-2), beginning on 5 December 1935. During the trials, project officer LT William V. Davis, assisted by LTJG George W. Anderson and LT Stewart H. Ingerson made a total of thirteen arrested landings and deck takeoffs with the XTBD-1. They reported that the XTBD-1 was an excellent aircraft for carrier operations.

The Great Lakes TG-2 was the standard torpedo bomber in service with the Fleet during 1937 and was replaced by the TBD-1. This aircraft served with VT-2 aboard USS LEXINGTON (CV-2). (National Archives)

After completing initial testing with the prototype, the Navy ordered a number of modifications to the XTBD-1. The canopy was changed to a higher canopy to improve crew headroom, visibility, and to provide room for an internal roll-over pylon. The oil cooler was relocated from the underside of the engine cowling to a new position under the starboard wing. The carburetor air intake on the port side of the cowling was deleted. The tail wheel was changed from a retractable unit to a fixed tail wheel.

Flight tests revealed a top speed of nearly 200 mph (clean) and a cruising speed of 120 mph with a full bomb load and 100 mph when carrying the Mk XIII torpedo. Range was 435 miles with the torpedo and 700 miles when armed with bombs. Service ceiling was 19,700 feet.

Finally on 16 January 1936, the XTBD-1 was accepted by the Navy, and on 3 February 1936, the aircraft was ordered into production under the designation TBD-1, with an initial contract for 114 aircraft (BuNos 0268 through 0381). The prototype was retained and used as a test-bed aircraft by the Navy, Douglas and Pratt & Whitney. On 21 March 1941, the prototype was transferred to NAS Norman, Oklahoma for use as a ground instructional airframe, where it remained until finally scrapped on 29 October 1943.

The XTBD-1 (BuNo 9720) prototype on a test flight during 1935. The XTBD-1 was the first all metal, low-wing monoplane to be accepted by the Navy for service aboard aircraft carriers. The main wheels were partially exposed when retracted to protect the fuselage underside in case of an emergency wheels up landing. (U.S. Navy)

During late 1935, the XTBD-1 underwent a number of modifications dictated by its initial testing. The canopy was changed to a taller canopy to improve pilot visibility and a roll-over pylon was added immediately behind the pilot's seat. The oil cooler was also repositioned from under the cowling to under the starboard wing. (National Archives)

The XTBG-1 was the Great Lakes entry in the torpedo bomber competition. It was the last biplane torpedo bomber considered by the Navy and had a top speed of 200 mph. It carried a crew of three with the torpedoman occupying the small front cockpit. (National Archives)

Development

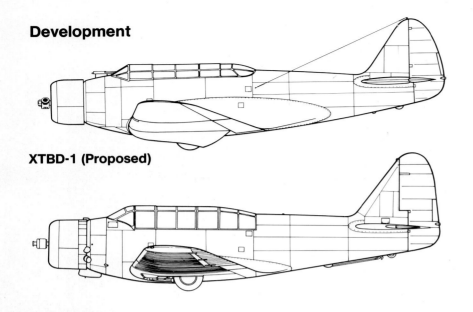

XTBD-1 (Proposed)

XTBD-1 (Early)

XTBD-1 (Late)

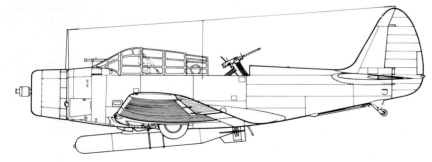

TBD-1 (Early)

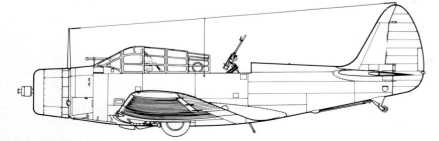

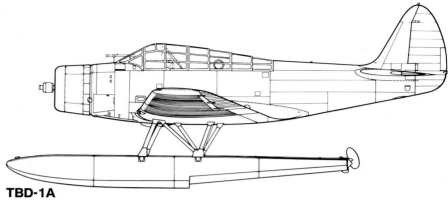

TBD-1A

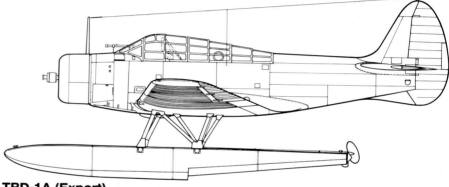

TBD-1A (Export)

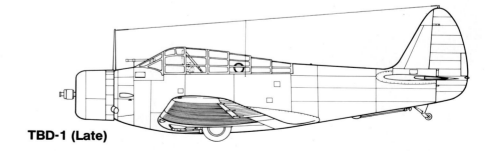

TBD-1 (Late)

TBD-1

The first production TBD-1 made its factory test flight during early May 1937 from the Douglas Santa Monica facility and was delivered to the Navy at Anacosta Naval Air Station on 27 June for acceptance. Externally, the aircraft differed very little from the modified prototype. It had the taller canopy and roll-over pylon. The 800 hp Pratt & Whitney XR-1830-60 engine was replaced with a production 900 hp R-1830-64 engine driving a three blade Hamilton Standard ten foot three inch constant speed propeller. The lower cowling was reshaped slightly to fair more smoothly into the lower fuselage and the vertical tail surfaces were enlarged to provide for greater stability and increased rudder control. The first two aircraft off the production line, BuNos 0268 and 0269 were retained by the Navy for test purposes.

When it first entered service, the TBD-1 was the most modern torpedo bomber in service with any navy and set a number of "firsts" for the Navy. It was the first all metal, low-wing torpedo bomber to join the inventory. At the time of its introduction into the Fleet, it was the most modern aircraft in either the Navy or the U.S. Army Air Corps. It carried the first torpedo designed specifically to be carried and launched by an aircraft. This torpedo, the Bliss-Leavitt Mk XIII, was eighteen inches in diameter, fifteen feet long and weighed 2,000 pounds. It was the first Navy aircraft to feature hydraulic folding wings that could be controlled by the pilot without leaving the aircraft. The wing fold was controlled from inside the aircraft by a control valve which was located on the starboard cockpit bulkhead.

By 1937 standards, the TBD-1 was very large for a carrier based aircraft. It had a length of thirty-five feet and a height of fifteen feet one inch. Its corrugated aluminum skin fifty foot wing, while very large, gave the TBD-1 outstanding low speed handling characteristics. Thanks to its light wing loading, the landing speed of the TBD-1 was only 63 mph. The light wing loading also gave the TBD-1 excellent maneuverability. Pilots reported that the TBD-1 could perform all the aerobatic maneuvers that the power would allow, including loops and rolls. Pilots also reported that with a full load the TBD-1s controls were somewhat heavy and unresponsive.

As an aid to ditching, each wing also contained an inflatable rubberized floatation bag designed to keep the aircraft afloat long enough for the crew to safely escape. The floatation bags were activated either manually by the pilot/assistant pilot or automatically. The bags were inflated by a CO_2 cylinder mounted in the assistant pilot's cockpit. Each wing also contained a single non-self sealing fuel tank for a total capacity of 207 gallons.

Armament for the TBD-1 consisted of a fixed M2 Browning .30 caliber machine gun mounted in the starboard side of the cowling and a flexible M2 Browning mounted on a ring mount in the rear cockpit for the gunner. When not in use, the flexible gun was stowed in a flap-covered trough to the rear of the gunner's cockpit. Aiming of the pilot's gun was done through a Mk IV telescopic gunsight which protruded through the lower portion of the front windscreen. The TBD-1 could also carry a Browning M2 .50 caliber machine gun as an alternative to the cowl mounted .30 caliber gun. It was not uncommon to find some aircraft in each squadron armed with the .50 caliber gun, while others were armed with the .30 caliber weapon.

Externally the TBD-1 could carry a variety of weapons, depending on the mission. For torpedo attack, either the Mk XIII or Mk VII-28 torpedo could be carried on the centerline rack. For bombing missions the TBD-1 could be fitted with up to twelve 100 pound bombs on underwing racks. Two Mk XXXV streamlined bomb racks were installed under the fuselage, one on either side of the centerline torpedo rack. These

This TBD-1 (BuNo 0268) was the first production TBD to roll off the assembly line at the Douglas Santa Monica, California plant. The aircraft was delivered to NAS Anacosta on 27 June 1937 and was formally accepted for service on 3 August 1937. It was retained by the Navy for experimental work and was never assigned to a squadron. (National Archives.)

Canopy Development

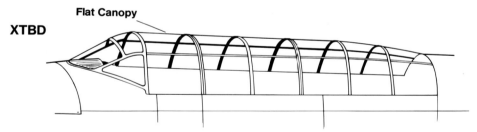

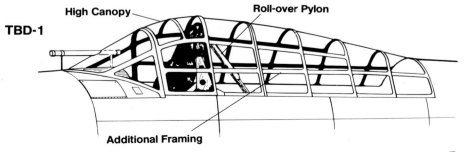

(Below) The TBD-1 was the first Navy aircraft to feature hydraulic folding wings. The outer thirteen feet of each wing folded up over the cockpit. The wings could be folded from inside the aircraft by either the pilot or assistant pilot/torpedoman. (U.S. Navy)

(Above) These TBD-1 are having the canopy, cockpit wiring, flotation bags, and other equipment installed at production stations fourteen and fifteen. The next position was station sixteen where the folding outer wing panels would be fitted. (McDonnell Douglas Aircraft)

racks could accommodate either 500 or 1,000 pound bombs. For level bombing, a Norden bomb sight was mounted in the fuselage below the pilot. The bombardier used the sight by lying prone in the belly and aiming through the bomb sight window. When the sight was not in use, the bomb sight windows were covered by two doors, which opened downward. Torpedo aiming was done by the pilot through his telescopic gun sight, with the torpedo director controls being mounted in the cockpit, just below the gun sight.

The long heavily framed green house canopy of the TBD-1 consisted of seven sections, four of which were movable. It was normal practice for the crew to conduct all takeoffs and landings with the canopy open. This was done primarily to allow for a fast exit in the event of a ditching or crash landing. In normal operations it was not uncommon for the TBD-1 to be flown with the canopy front and rear sections open.

On 16 August 1938, the Navy ordered an additional fifteen TBD-1s to replace aircraft lost in training and to provide additional aircraft for new squadrons being formed. These aircraft, BuNos 1505 through 1519, differed slightly from the earlier production TBD-1s. The wing walk areas on late production TBD-1s were doubled in size from nine and one half inches to eighteen and one half inches. One of the indentification/formation lights on the tail was relocated from its position on the port horizontal stabilizer to a new position at the front base of the vertical stabilizer.

The TBD-1 officially entered squadron service when the third production aircraft (BuNo 0270) was delivered to Torpedo Squadron Three (VT-3) aboard USS SARATOGA (CV-3) on 5 October 1937.

(Below) The TBD-1 production line at Santa Monica during January of 1938 shows fourteen TBD-1s in various stages of construction. Aircraft that were scheduled to be delivered to various fleet squadrons were marked with the proper codes and colors before leaving the factory. The aircraft in the left foreground are destined for VT-2 aboard USS LEXINGTON. (McDonnell Douglas Aircraft)

(Above) This TBD-1 (BuNo 0308) is undergoing landing gear drop tests at the Douglas factory. The aircraft will be delivered to VT-2 aboard USS LEXINGTON and carries the squadron insignia on the fuselage below the cockpit, along with the squadron code, 2-T-15, in Black on the rear fuselage sides. (McDonnell Douglas Aircraft)

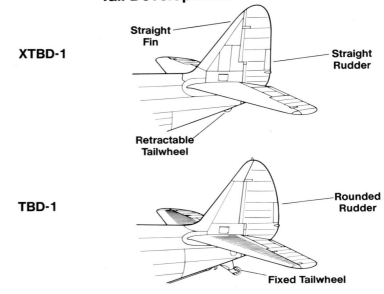

Tail Development

XTBD-1

Straight Fin

Straight Rudder

Retractable Tailwheel

TBD-1

Rounded Rudder

Fixed Tailwheel

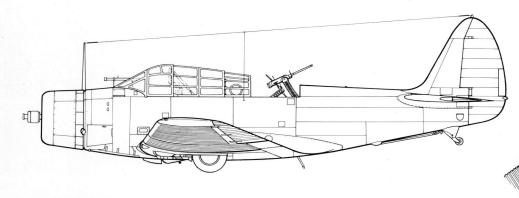

Specifications

Douglas TBD-1 Devastator

Wingspan . . . . 50 feet
Length . . . . 35 feet
Height . . . . 15 feet 1 inch
Empty Weight . . . . 6,182 pounds
Maximum Weight . . . . 9,862 pounds
Powerplant . . . . One 900 hp Pratt & Whitney
R-1830-64 radial engine

Armament . . . . Either one .30 caliber or one .50
caliber machine gun in the star-
board nose and one .30 caliber
machine gun in the rear cockpit.
One Mk XIII Torpedo or
1,200 pounds of bombs.

Performance
  Maximum Speed . . . . 206 mph
  Service ceiling . . . . 19,700 feet
  Range . . . . 700 miles
Crew . . . . Three

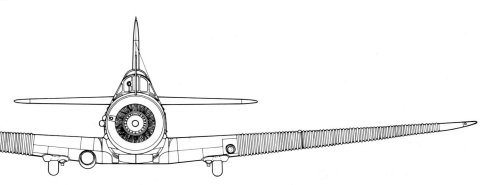

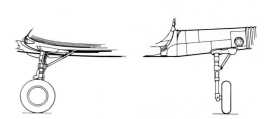

The forward firing machine gun carried on the TBD-1 was either a Browning .30 or .50 caliber machine gun. The gun mount was dampened to reduce the vibration when the gun was fired, and the spent shell casings were ejected through the chute just below the gun. (National Archives)

Cowling

XTBD-1

- Venturi
- Small Intake
- Small Air Intake
- Gun port
- Oil Cooler

TBD-1

- Larger Intake
- Intake Deleted
- Repositioned Oil Cooler
- Revised Lower Fuselage Contour

The pilot's Mk III, Model 2 telescopic gun sight was mounted in the windshield ahead of the pilot, and had a simple ring and bead sight mounted above it. This sight was used when firing the cowling mounted machine gun. Immediately below it is the Mk XXIV torpedo director. (National Archives)

The Mk III, Model 2 telescopic gunsight had a rubber eyepiece to protect the pilot. The Mk XXIV torpedo director sight was operated by estimating the target's size, speed, and distance. When entered into the sight, these figures would give the pilot the proper release point. (McDonnell Douglas Aircraft)

The fully adjustable pilot's seat on the TBD-1 was made of aluminum. The port side cockpit panel contained the throttle, arresting hook control, trim controls, and fuel controls. Early TBD-1s had the cockpit painted in Aluminum dope, while later aircraft were painted in Green Zink Chromate. (McDonnell Douglas Aircraft)

Two folding doors covered the bomb sight window when the sight was not being used. The bombardier controlled the doors with a crank handle located on the bombardier's control panel. (McDonnell Douglas Aircraft)

The assistant pilot/bombardier's cockpit was immediately behind the pilot's cockpit. The gas cylinder to the right of the seat is the CO_2 cylinder for inflating the wing flotation bags. The seats in the TBD-1 were designed to hold seat type parachute packs which also doubled as seat cushions. (McDonnell Douglas Aircraft)

TBD-1s carried the Norden Mark XV-3 computing bomb sight for use on level bombing missions. The sight was mounted below the pilot's position and the bombardier used the sight while lying prone in the belly of the TBD. (McDonnell Douglas Aircraft)

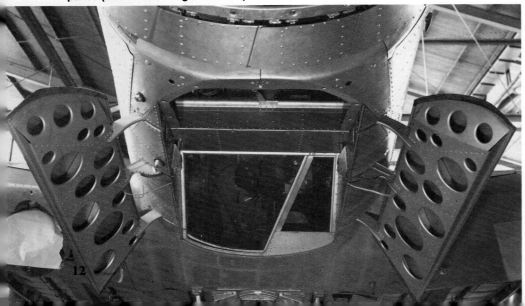

The radioman/gunner's position featured a ring type gun mount for a Browning .30 caliber machine gun. The radio equipment was installed in the forward portion of the cockpit on the panels marked for their installation. (McDonnell Douglas Aircraft)

The rear Browning.30 caliber machine gun was fitted with a flexible windage type forward gun sight and a flash arrester. When not in use the gun could be stowed in a slot located immediately behind the gun which was covered by two downward folding doors. (National Archives)

The standard weapon fitted to the gunners position of the TBD-1 was the Browning .30 caliber machine gun with 600 rounds of ammunition. The gunner's seat moved with the gun mount 180° horizontally, 90° vertically and rotated a full 360°. (McDonnell Douglas Aircraft)

13

TBD-1A

The Navy had expressed an interest in the TBD as a sea based patrol aircraft and on 21 June 1939, the first production TBD-1 (BuNo 0268) was ferried to the Naval Aircraft Factory, located at the Philadelphia Navy Yard, for the installation of a pair of EDO floats. The EDO Corporation, named for Earl Dodge Osborn, had been making floats for the Navy since 1925 and had a reputation for building lightweight, sturdy, aluminum floats for a variety of uses. The twin float installation on the TBD-1 was completed on 14 August 1939 and the aircraft was re-designated by the Navy as the TBD-1A.

The TBD-1A was basically a TBD-1 with the landing gear replaced by an EDO steerable twin float installation. In order to support the weight of the TBD-1 and the 2,000 pound Mk XIII torpedo, the twin floats used on the TBD-1A were the largest ever fitted to a single engined aircraft. The floats were some twenty-nine feet long and were connected to the TBD-1 with an extensive system of aluminum struts. To allow the aircraft to be beached for maintenance, a special wheeled dolly was designed and built by EDO. During the modification of the TBD-1 to floats, the tail wheel and arresting hook were removed and the tail wheel position faired over. To aid the crew in boarding the aircraft, a grab handle was installed on the starboard wingroot, near the wing trailing edge.

Initial testing of the TBD-1A was done at NAS Anacostia, Washington, D.C. After one month of preliminary tests, the aircraft was transferred to NAS Gould Island, Newport, Rhode Island for additional testing. These early tests showed that the float installation caused no adverse effects on the flight characteristics of the TBD-1A, except for a 20 mph loss of speed (which was to be expected). Test pilots also reported that the water handling of the TBD-1A was good.

During 1939, a variant of the TBD-1A was proposed to the government of the Netherlands for use as a coastal patrol bomber. Known as the *De Vliegende Hollander* (Flying Dutchman) the proposed TBD-1A variant was to be equipped with a 1,200 hp Pratt & Whitney GR-1820-G105A engine, the same engine the Dutch had specified for installation on the Brewster Buffalo fighters that were being purchased by Holland. Additionally, the Dutch specified that the rudder area was to be increased. The German invasion of Holland in May of 1940 ended negotiations and when Douglas could not interest the Navy or any other foreign buyer in the TBD-1A, the project was cancelled.

During 1940, the TBD-1A was overhauled at the Naval Aircraft Factory and returned to NAS Gould Island for a series of special armament tests on the Mk XIII torpedo. The Navy had been experiencing a number of problems with the torpedos, such as breaking up on impact with the water and sounding (diving to the bottom). The TBD-1A's slow speed and stable handling made it an ideal platform to conduct the tests. The torpedo tests ran from May of 1942 until May of 1943, under the control of Experimental Squadron Two and the 1st Naval District. As a result of these tests a number of improvements were made to the Mk XIII; however, the torpedo never really lived up to its potential until much later, when the California Institute of Technology devised a special ring tail shroud for the Mk XIII which greatly improved its flight characteristics.

Later the TBD-1A was also used to conduct a series of tests on a revised wing intended for service TBD-1s and for tests of improved radio equipment. After some six years of service as a test bed, the TBD-1A was retired from the Navy on 22 September 1943 and scrapped the next day. For most of its service career, the TBD-1A operated on floats, the only TBD to be so equipped.

The TBD-1A is prepared for launch by the beach crew. The man in the long white coat is a representative of the Naval Aircraft Factory. The TBD-1A had grab handles added to the wing upper surface near the wing trailing edge to aid the crew in boarding the aircraft. (National Archives)

Plane handlers move the boarding ladder into position so the pilot and observer can man the TBD-1A at New Port, Rhode Island Naval Base. The base was located on Coasters Harbor, a protected harbor perfect for torpedo tests. The TBD-1A was used for torpedo tests between 1939 and 1943. (National Archives).

The TBD-1A taxies out in preparation for a flight test during 1940. At the time the TBD-1A was built, its EDO floats were the largest ever fitted to a single engine aircraft. (McDonnell Douglas Aircraft)

The TBD-1A on its beaching gear on the seaplane ramp of the Naval Torpedo Station at NAF Gould Island, during late 1939. The aircraft was a one of a kind prototype and was used for various test programs. The float installation reduced the aircraft's top speed by 20 mph. (CAPT W.E.Scarborough)

Float Installation

TBD-1A

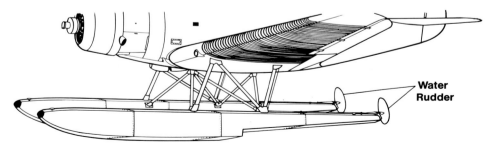

Water Rudder

(Above) Torpedomen prepare a Bliss-Leavitt Mk XIII torpedo for loading onto its handling dolly. The Mk XIII had to be released at an altitude no higher than 100 feet and at an airspeed no greater than 120 mph. The Mk XIII proved to be prone to problems and suffered a great many failures in combat. (National Archives)

(Above) The TBD-1A launches a Mk XIII torpedo during drop tests held at NAF Gould Island. The smoke trail behind the torpedo is the exhaust from the alcohol powered motor. Because of its slow speed and stability, the TBD-1A was a perfect test platform. (U.S. Navy)

(Right) The float equipped TBD-1A on the ramp at NAF Gould Island, Newport, Rhode Island during late 1939. The TBD-1A was a standard TBD-1 fitted with EDO floats. The fuselage marking, 2X^D1 stood for Experimental Squadron 2, 1st Naval District, aircraft number 1. (CAPT W.E. Scarborough via San Diego Aero Space Museum)

Into Service

During the Fall of 1937, the U.S. Navy was operating five aircraft carriers (CVs). The air groups aboard four of these, USS SARATOGA (CV-3), USS LEXINGTON (CV-2), USS YORKTOWN (CV-5), and USS ENTERPRISE (CV-6) would be re-equipped with the TBD-1. The fifth, USS RANGER, was originally believed to have too short a flight deck to operate the TBD-1 (although she would later receive a small number of them).

The first unit to re-equip with the TBD-1 was VT-3 aboard USS SARATOGA which received its first aircraft on 5 October 1937. Within two months, the squadron had built up to its full complement of eighteen TBD-1s organized into six elements of three aircraft each (numbered 3-T-1 through 3-T-18). VT-3 became the pioneer TBD unit and uncovered some of the bugs in the aircraft during early service use. The wing fold system caused a number of problems. Care had to be taken to ensure that the wing fold locking pins were in place before taking off. The locks could be checked visually from the cockpit with the aid of a pair of wing fold lock flags which protruded from the upper surface of the wing if the locks were not properly secured. One young pilot apparently forgot this item on his check list and, upon takeoff, one wing began to fold. The aircraft rolled to port and impacted into the ground, killing the pilot.

During 1937, VT-3 took part in the annual Fleet exercise. The squadron launched from SARATOGA some 100 miles out of Pearl Harbor, Hawaii, and successfully attacked the ships in the harbor and shore installations at Ford Island. The tactics used by VT-3 were very similar to those that would be employed by the Japanese some four years later. Shortly after the conclusion of the war games, VT-3 encountered salt corrosion in the wings of its TBD-1s and the entire squadron had to have new wing skinning installed during early 1938.

The second squadron to receive TBDs was VT-2 aboard USS LEXINGTON. By April of 1938, the squadron had received its full strength of twenty-one TBDs. VT-5 aboard USS YORKTOWN followed in February of 1938 and, by June, the squadron had been fully re-equipped with twenty TBDs.

Carrier operations, even in peacetime, are hazardous operations and accidents soon reduced the number of available TBDs from 129 down to 100. With two new carriers about to enter service, USS HORNET (CV-8) and USS WASP (CV-7), the Navy decided to order an additional fifteen TBDs from Douglas. These aircraft would be used to replace the losses suffered during training.

A single TBD was also used by the Marine Corps Base Air Detachment Two (BAD-2) at NAS North Island, California. It received TBD-1 BuNo 1518, and operated the aircraft for a short period before transferring it to VMS-2 on 26 March 1941. The TBD served with VMS-2 as a target tug, scout trainer and squadron hack until 5 June 1941, when it was returned to the Navy. The aircraft was used by VT-3 and VT-6 for short periods before being transferred to VT-8 aboard USS HORNET on 29 April 1942. The aircraft was assigned to one of the unit's young pilots, ENS George Gay.

The war in Europe prompted the Navy to begin planning for the formation of two additional TBD squadrons. Both of these squadrons, however, did not reach operational status until after the Japanese attack on Pearl Harbor. VT-4 aboard USS RANGER was declared operational on 17 December 1941 and VT-7 aboard USS WASP was formally commissioned on 26 December. Originally thought to be too small to operate the TBD, USS RANGER not only had VT-4 aboard, but also operated VS-41, a scouting unit flying TBDs in the bombing role. Two other scouting squadrons, VS-71 and VS-72, also operated TBDs alongside their SB2U Vindicators. One Utility Squadron, VJ-3, also operated a single TBD (BuNo 0342) for a short period from 19 March to 4 April 1940 aboard the fleet repair ship USS RIGEL (AR-11).

During August and September of 1940 the Navy painted a number of aircraft in the experimental Barclay camouflage. This multi-color, multi-shape camouflage was designed to confuse enemy gunners as to the the the aircraft's direction of flight, size and distance at extreme ranges. A number of TBDs from VT-2 and VT-3 were painted in the experimental camouflage for fleet trials. After the trials ended in late Fall of 1940, all aircraft had the paint stripped off and they were returned to their original finish. The Barclay camouflage was found to be ineffective; however, the data gained from these tests helped the Navy devise the camouflage schemes that would be used during the Second World War.

On 1 October 1941, the Secretary of the Navy issued an order officially naming the TBD-1 the Devastator. The names issued to Navy aircraft during this period were all designed to show potential enemies the resolve of the American people. Other names issued during this time period included Dauntless for the Douglas SBD dive bomber, and Wildcat for the Grumman F4F fighter.

The Naval Air Training Command also used ten TBDs as advanced trainers at NAS Pensacola, Florida. The first TBDs arrived at the NATC during 1938. These aircraft were finished at the factory in overall Aluminum dope with various colored cowlings and fuselage striping to give them the appearance of active duty squadron aircraft. For the most part, these ten aircraft (less losses) would continue in the training role throughout the war years. For brief periods a number were borrowed by fleet units (such as VT-4, VT-5, VT-8, VS-42, and VS-71) to fill out a squadron's organization while on Atlantic patrols. Once the patrol was completed, the aircraft were returned to the training command. After the Battle of Midway in June of 1942, all remaining TBDs in the inventory were transferred to the Training Command. These aircraft served at Chicago, Pensacola, Norfolk, and Miami. A number were used to conduct carrier qualifications aboard the USS LONG ISLAND and USS CHARGER, converted side wheel passenger steamers in the Great Lakes. These training Devastators continued in service until November of 1944 when the Navy ordered the last of the TBDs to be retired from Naval service.

This TBD-1 (BuNo 0273) was accepted by the Navy on 26 October 1938 and assigned to Torpedo Squadron Three (VT-3) aboard USS SARATOGA (CV-3). The aircraft was overall Aluminum dope with Orange Yellow wing uppersurfaces, a White tail, and Blue lower cowling band. (Smithsonian Institution)

TBDs of the third section of Torpedo Squadron Five (VT-5) fly formation over California during 1940. 5-T-7 has the twenty inch wide True Blue fuselage band indicating it as the section leader's aircraft. VT-5 was stationed aboard the USS YORKTOWN (CV-5). (United Technologies)

A deck crewman prepares to remove the wheel chocks from a TBD-1 of VT-3 aboard USS SARATOGA as the aircraft ahead of it (3-T-2) goes to full power for a deck launch. Deck crews had to be alert at all times to avoid being blown off the deck by the prop wash of maneuvering aircraft. (National Archives)

A TBD-1 of VT-3 at Oakland, California, during 1938. The aircraft has Orange Yellow wing uppersurfaces, with Willow Green wing chevron and upper half of the cowl band. The tail is White, the assigned color of USS SARATOGA. The squadron insignia was carried on the fuselage side just below the cockpit. (William T. Larkins)

TBD-1s of VT-6 on the ramp at Naval Air Station Sunnydale, California, during 1938. The tail, wing chevron, and upper cowling of 6-T-8 (BuNo 0329) are True Blue. BuNo 0329 would later serve with VT-3 aboard SARATOGA, VT-2 aboard LEXINGTON and finally VT-8 aboard HORNET. (William T. Larkins)

Alternate .50 Caliber Cowl Gun

.30 Caliber Gun Installation

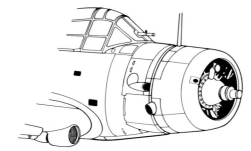

.50 Caliber Gun Installation

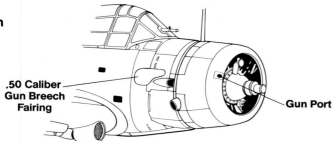

.50 Caliber Gun Breech Fairing

Gun Port

This early production TBD-1 (BuNo 0302) of VT-2 assigned to USS LEXINGTON carries a Lemon Yellow tail and top half of the cowling with Orange-Yellow wing uppersurfaces. The large fairing on the fuselage side just below the cockpit indicates that this TBD-1 is armed with a .50 caliber cowling gun in place of the smaller .30 caliber gun. (William T. Larkins)

TBD-1s of Torpedo Squadron Five (VT-5) aboard USS YORKTOWN fly formation over California during early 1940. The aircraft all have Red tails (the assigned color for USS YORKTOWN). The wing chevrons, cowl bands and fuselage band on 5-T-7 are True Blue, the section color for the third section. (U.S. Navy via W.T. Larkins)

5-T-7 (BuNo 0331) was flown by the leader of the squadron's third section and carried a section leader's fuselage band in True Blue and a Battle E award on the fuselage side in White. After being retired from the Fleet, BuNo 0331 served as a trainer at Dahlgren, Virginia until late 1944. (National Archives)

TBD-1s of Torpedo Squadron Two (VT-2) in a right echelon formation over California during early 1941. The aircraft carry a Red E on the fuselage side indicating the squadron had been awarded an excellence in gunnery award and the tails are White. (U.S. Navy)

This TBD-1 (BuNo 0331) served with VT-5 from 1938 until 1941 when she was transferred to VT-7 aboard USS WASP. After serving a tour aboard WASP, she was assigned as a trainer until she was finally scrapped on 9 August 1944. At that time, BuNo 0331 was one the last TBDs left in the Navy. (Smithsonian Institution)

A TBD-1 of VT-3 comes in for a landing aboard USS SARATOGA (CV-3). The landing signal officer (LSO) has just given the pilot the cut signal for him to chop his throttle. The TBD-1 had a landing speed of 63 mph, thanks to its light wing loading and large flaps. (National Archives)

TBD-1s of Torpedo Squadron Three (VT-3) line up for deck launch from USS SARATOGA (CV-3) during 1938. The squadron commander in 3-T-1 (BuNo 0279) is leading the group and is awaiting the takeoff signal from the flight deck officer in the foreground. (McDonnell Douglas Aircraft)

6-T-3 was the third aircraft of VT-6's first section and has the lower half of the cowling ring painted in Insignia Red. The TBD has the later style pitot type which had an air temperature gauge just ahead ot the wing leading edge. The Devastator also has the optional .50 caliber gun installation. (William T. Larkins)

This TBD-1 (BuNo 0360) was assigned to VT-5 as a replacement aircraft and was not carried on the original squadron inventory. Replacement aircraft were to be used when one of the squadron's other aircraft was pulled for maintenance or was lost. (U.S. Navy)

Pitot Tube

TBD-1 (Early)

TBD-1 (Late)

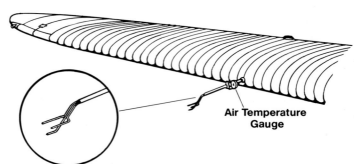

Air Temperature Gauge

22

(Below) This TBD-1 (BuNo 0358) suffered a hydraulic failure and made a water landing in Pensacola Bay on 15 August 1938. The flotation bags worked, and the aircraft was salvaged, repaired and later served with Torpedo Squadron Five (VT-5) in the Atlantic. (U.S. Navy)

(Above) A TBD-1 of VT-6 high over Coronado Bay, San Diego, California, has the cowling, wing chevron and fuselage band in Red while the tail is True Blue. All canopies are open, which was the usual practice when flying the TBD. (U.S. Navy)

This TBD-1 (BuNo 0344) of VT-6 was the second aircraft in the fifth section and has the upper cowling and wing chevron in Willow Green. She would later serve with VT-3 and VT-5 before being lost at sea on 25 May 1941. (William T. Larkins)

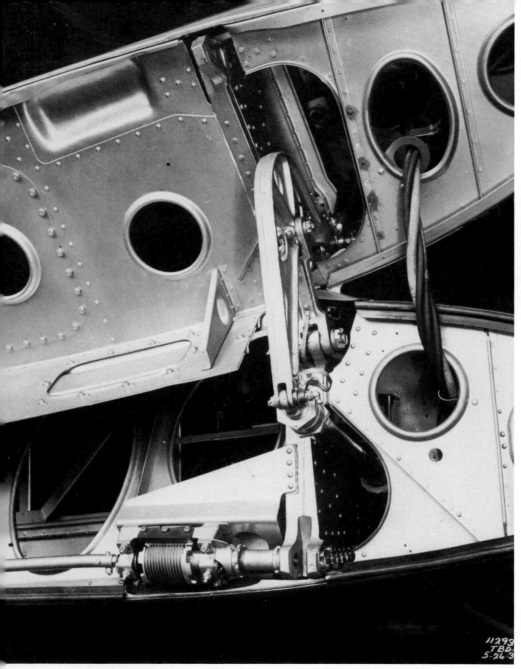

This TBD-1 (BuNo 0324) of VT-6 spreads its wings on the ramp before taxing out for takeoff. After his aircraft crashed during 1939, the commander of VT-6 took over BuNo 0324 as his aircraft and had it renumbered 6-T-1 with the original number being painted out with Aluminum paint. (William T. Larkins)

3-T-18 of VT-3 had a short operational career. She was officially accepted by the Navy on 17 December 1937 and seven months later, on 29 July 1938, she was lost when the TBD crashed, and was totally destroyed in the resulting fire. (William T. Larkins)

The wing fold of the TBD was secured in the down position by the wing fold locking pin (bottom). A number of accidents were caused during early TBD operations when ground crews forgot to engage the wing locking pin. (National Archives)

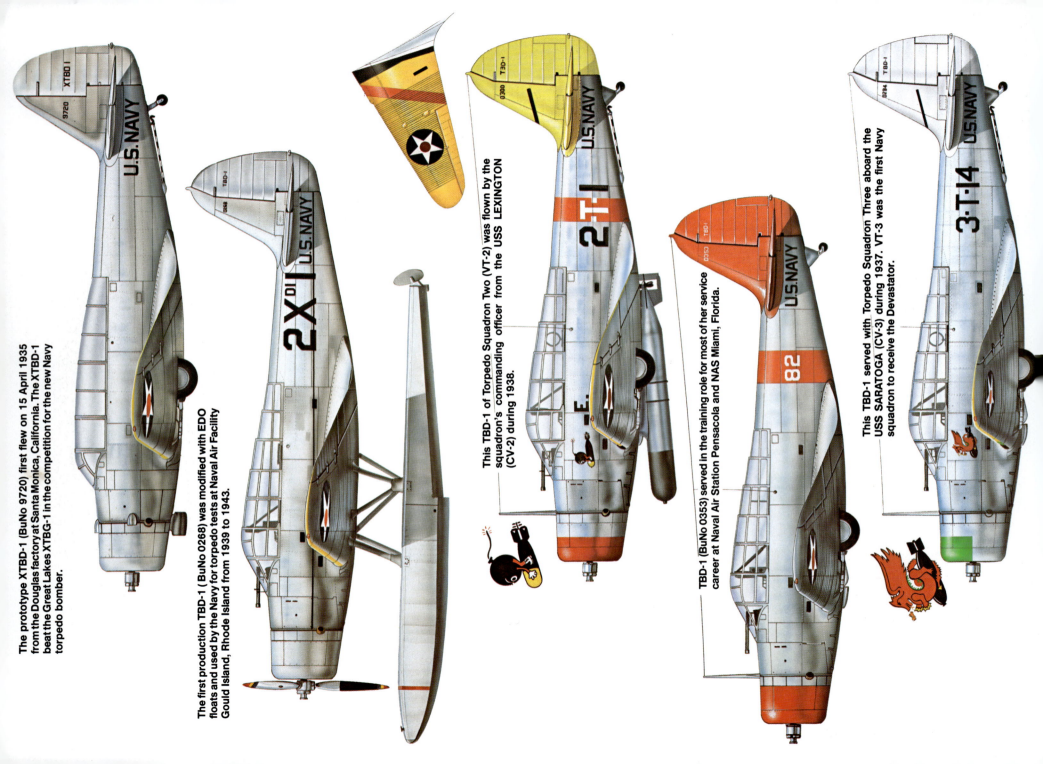

The prototype XTBD-1 (BuNo 9720) first flew on 15 April 1935 from the Douglas factory at Santa Monica, California. The XTBD-1 beat the Great Lakes XTBG-1 in the competition for the new Navy torpedo bomber.

The first production TBD-1 (BuNo 0268) was modified with EDO floats and used by the Navy for torpedo tests at Naval Air Facility Gould Island, Rhode Island from 1939 to 1943.

This TBD-1 of Torpedo Squadron Two (VT-2) was flown by the squadron's commanding officer from the USS LEXINGTON (CV-2) during 1938.

TBD-1 (BuNo 0353) served in the training role for most of her service career at Naval Air Station Pensacola and NAS Miami, Florida.

This TBD-1 served with Torpedo Squadron Three aboard the USS SARATOGA (CV-3) during 1937. VT-3 was the first Navy squadron to receive the Devastator.

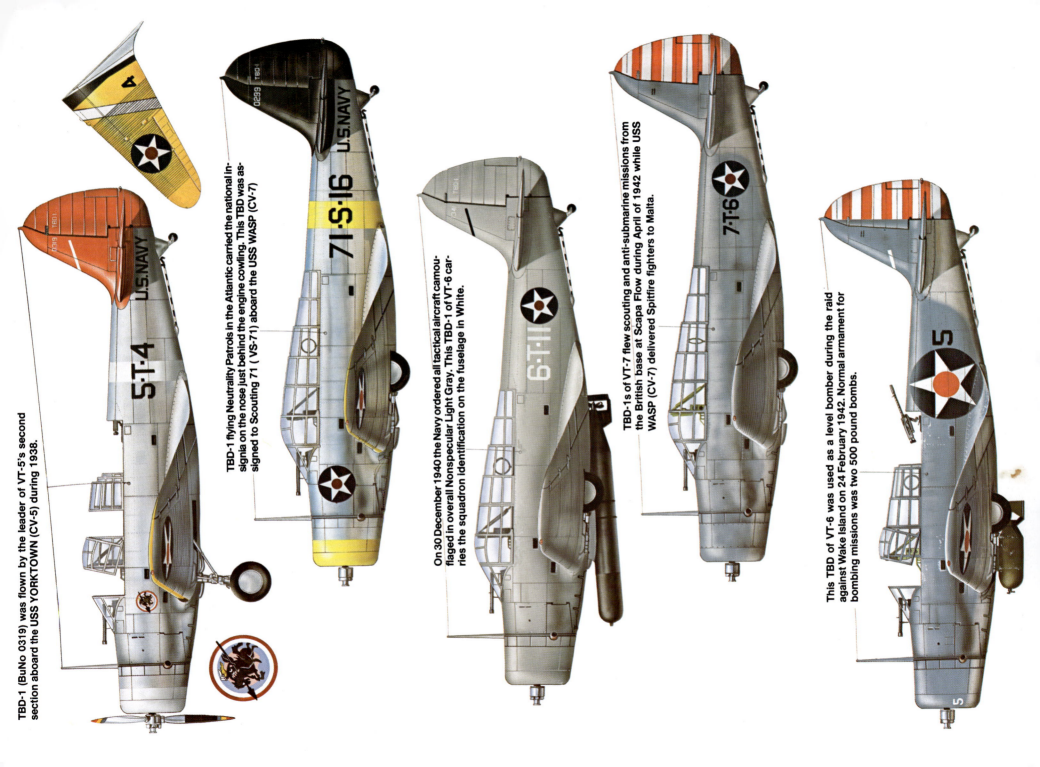

TBD-1 (BuNo 0319) was flown by the leader of VT-5's second section aboard the USS YORKTOWN (CV-5) during 1938.

TBD-1 flying Neutrality Patrols in the Atlantic carried the national insignia on the nose just behind the engine cowling. This TBD was assigned to Scouting 71 (VS-71) aboard the USS WASP (CV-7)

On 30 December 1940 the Navy ordered all tactical aircraft camouflaged in overall Nonspecular Light Gray. This TBD-1 of VT-6 carries the squadron identification on the fuselage in White.

TBD-1s of VT-7 flew scouting and anti-submarine missions from the British base at Scapa Flow during April of 1942 while USS WASP (CV-7) delivered Spitfire fighters to Malta.

This TBD of VT-6 was used as a level bomber during the raid against Wake Island on 24 February 1942. Normal armament for bombing missions was two 500 pound bombs.

TBD-1s of VT-6 are parked on the rear flight deck of USS ENTERPRISE (CV-6). Besides VT-6, the air group on ENTERPRISE consisted of VS-6 with Curtiss SBC-3s, VF-6 with Grumman F3Fs, and VB-6 with Northrup BT-1s. Only the TBDs would remain aboard when ENTERPRISE went to war. (National Archives)

A flight of six TBD-1 Devastators of Torpedo Squadron Six (VT-6) fly past Diamond Head, Hawaii during 1939. The aircraft have Orange-Yellow wings and Blue tails. The cowl band, fuselage band and wing chevrons were in various colors depending on the flight assignment within the squadron. (Naval Historical Center)

This Devastator (BuNo 0322) of Torpedo Squadron Six (VT-6) has the True Blue tail surfaces carried by all aircraft assigned to the carrier, USS ENTERPRISE (CV-6). (U.S. Navy)

(Above) Three TBDs of VT-5 (5-T-4, 5-T-17, and 5-T-16) prepare for takeoff from Oakland, California, during June of 1939. Both 5-T-16 and 5-T-17 were lost to crashes before the war and 5-T-4 would be transferred to VT-8 in time for the Battle of Midway. (William T. Larkins)

A TBD-1 of VT-2 flies over the USS ENTERPRISE during 1938. BuNo 0323 was later renumbered 6-T-1 when the original 6-T-1 crashed. The aircraft carries a small turtle emblem on the fin indicating the crew had crossed the equator, becoming Shellbacks. (National Archives)

(Below) TBD-1s of VT-3 and VT-6 took part in the making of the Warner Brothers movie *Hell Diver* during 1941. The aircraft were filmed at Naval Air Station Sunnydale, California. VT-3's TBDs still carried the colorful prewar markings while those of VT-6 were camouflaged in the Non-specular Light Gray. The aircraft overhead are BG-1s of VMB-2. (National Archives)

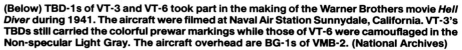

This TBD-1 (BuNo 0320) of VT-2 was painted in the experimental Barclay Design 7 camouflage scheme which was designed to confuse enemy gunners at extreme range. The aircraft was later lost in combat during the Battle of the Coral Sea. (USN/ B. Cressman via Jim Mesko)

The Barclay scheme differed on each side of the aircraft. The colors are believed to be Black, Silver Gray and Mid-Gray. (USN/B. Cressman via Jim Mesko)

This Devastator (BuNo 0339) of VT-3 assigned to USS SARATOGA carried the Barclay Design 8 pattern. The camouflage paints used were water based and weathered rapidly. (USN/B. Cressman via Jim Mesko)

After the fleet trials were completed, 0339 had the paint stripped off and was returned to its original finish. The Barclay camouflage was found to be ineffective and the tests were terminated in the late Fall of 1940. 0339 was later transferred to VT-2 and was lost in the Coral Sea during May of 1942. (USN/B. Cressman via Jim Mesko)

Combat

By late 1940, events in Europe made it obvious that sooner or later the United States would become involved in the war. The Battle of Britain and the Japanese signing of the Axis Pact with Germany and Italy convinced President Roosevelt to strengthen our carrier fleets. Earlier, in October of 1939, he had ordered the U.S. Pacific Fleet to relocate from its home port at San Diego, California to Pearl Harbor Hawaii in order to shorten the steaming time to our bases in the Pacific.

In the Atlantic, Neutrality Patrols were being conducted as a "show the flag" measure. Originally the TBDs on Neutrality Patrol were flown in their pre-war finish of overall Aluminum Dope with Chrome Yellow wing uppersurfaces and various colored cowlings and tail surfaces. The only special marking was the application of the U.S. national insignia to the cowling or forward fuselage as an identification aid. As the international situation worsened, the Navy decided to introduce camouflage on all carrier-based aircraft. BuAer ordered that all ship based aircraft would be camouflaged in an overall Non-specular Light Gray.

As the U.S. Navy moved closer to a war footing, orders were issued to modify squadron TBDs by removing the wing floatation bags. This was a security measure, designed to prevent any ditched TBD from falling into "enemy" hands. Other field modifications were performed on a number of TBDs. VT-6 modified their Devasators with dual Automatic Direction Finding antennas, with the second antenna running from the tail to the roll-over pylon.

When the Japanese attacked Pearl Harbor on 7 December 1941, none of the Pacific Fleet carriers (LEXINGTON, SARATOGA, and ENTERPRISE) were in port and within two months, these ships were carrying the war to the enemy. The first offensive action by the Pacific Fleet carriers were raids against the Japanese bases at Kwajalein, Jaluit, and Taroa, islands in the Marshall and Gilbert Islands chains. TBDs of VT-6 aboard ENTERPRISE hit Kwajalein on 1 February 1942, attacking ships in the harbor, while VT-5 aboard USS YORKTOWN attacked Jaluit the same morning. Problems with the Mk XIII torpedos kept the raids from being a complete success. At Kwajalein, VT-6 sunk one armed trawler and damaged seven other ships, without loss to the squadron. Later that day VT-6 returned to Kwajalein armed with 500 pound bombs and attacked the airfield and oil storage areas. Although significant damage was done to the base facilities and a number of oil tanks were destroyed, the airfield remained operational

VT-5 from USS YORKTOWN attacked shipping at Jaluit, losing four TBDs during the attack. Two were ditched in Jaluit harbor after running out of fuel. LT Harlan Johnson, HCMM Charles Fosha and RM1 Dalzell crewed 5-T-10 (BuNo 0298) and LTJG H.R. Heing with AD3 Starbl and First Class Radioman Striker Weindham crewed BuNo 1515. LT Johnson (later Admiral Johnson) recalled the mission.

Jaluit was scheduled as a maximum distance raid and was then launched early due to weather. The decision to launch the TBDs was made despite the fact that the ship was running away from us at 25 knots and also despite the fact that SBDs, which had a vastly longer range than the TBDs, were available. We flew over the first (eastern) chain of islands in the Jaluit Atoll in the soup and did not see them. We were flying on instruments below 500 feet, trailing about 300 feet of antenna wire as an early warning of being too low. We stayed on course ten to fifteen minutes beyond our assigned departure time looking for the target, which did not exist. Turned away from the islands into the surf put me on an incoming course. Fosha soon advised me of the error and I reversed course. After we reached the eastern chain of islands, I recalculated our time of arrival at the ship and determined that we would be fifty to seventy-five miles short. We continued on towards the ship until we found some SBDs that were headed

TBD-1s of VT-3 line up for takeoff from the USS SARATOGA during early 1941. The aircraft carry the overall Non-specular Light Gray camouflage adopted by the Navy in December of 1940. In addition to the new camouflage, the TBDs now carry a small national insignia on the fuselage side. (United Technologies Archives)

home and I was able wave off the SBDs that had joined on us earlier. Since the *YORKTOWN* did not have any destroyers attached to serve as rescue ships at the time of our departure, and since I did not think that they would risk a cruiser to pick us up, I canvassed the crews as to their desires. Should we land in the water at Jaluit and attempt to commandeer a boat for our escape, or should we float around the Pacific and hope for rescue? They all agreed, try Jaluit. I broke radio silence and informed the ship that I would ditch at Jaluit unless otherwise advised. When we received no word from the ship, we turned back and ditched at Jaluit.

After jettisoning their bombs, the two aircraft made smooth water landings in the lagoon about 100 yards apart. Both crews managed to make it to shore, but were later captured by the Japanese, spending the rest of the war as POWs. The other two VT-6 aircraft lost were destroyed in a mid-air collision.

Other raids followed. Wake Island was hit by VT-6 aboard ENTERPRISE on 24 February 1942, then hit Marcus Island on 4 March. The largest raid was a two ship effort against Lae and Salamaua on New Guinea. LEXINGTON and YORKTOWN launched their air groups forty-five miles off the New Guinea coast with the aircraft crossing the Owen Stanley mountains to achieve complete surprise on the two Japanese bases. Unfortunately, the largest target in either harbor was an old light cruiser. Of the twenty-three torpedos dropped by VT-2 and VT-5, only one hit was scored (a 6,000 ton transport). It was the same old story of defective torpedos and warhead exploders. The raids, however, were an important morale boost to the American public when they were reported in the press under the banner headlines; *Pearl Harbor Avenged.*

These raids revealed the short comings of the TBD in speed and range and the problems with the Mk XIII torpedo. They also led many senior officials to believe that the TBD could still be an effective weapon. During the raids, the Devastator had not faced intense fighter reaction from the Japanese and had the benefit of friendly fighter cover. Without these two advantages, the results would be far different as events would soon reveal.

On 30 December 1940, the Navy ordered all tactical aircraft camouflaged in overall Nonspecular Light Gray. These TBDs of VT-6 carry the new color scheme with the aircraft numbers on the fuselage sides painted in White. (National Archives)

Hook down and landing gear down, a TBD-1 of VT-3 begins its approach to USS SARATOGA, passing over a MARYLAND class battleship during one of the neutrality patrols of 1941. Normally during these patrols the TBDs were used as scout aircraft and did not carry torpedos. (National Archives)

(Above) A TBD-1 of VT-3 enters the landing pattern for USS SARATOGA (CV-3) while on neutrality patrol during October of 1941. The camouflage was particularly effective in the North Atlantic patrol areas, blending into the gray of the low winter clouds. (U.S. Navy via United Technologies Archives)

(Below) TBD-1s painted in the Non-specular Light Gray camouflage were very drab in comparison to the colorful pre-war markings used on the TBDs. Small sized national insignia was carried on the fuselage sides, upper port and lower starboard wing and all lettering was in White. (National Archives)

Ground crewmen position a TBD of VT-8 on the ramp at Naval Air Station Norfolk, Virginia during late 1941. The aircraft carries the new camouflage scheme of Non-specular Blue Gray uppersurfaces over Non-specular Light Gray undersurfaces with Red and White rudder stripes. (National Archives)

A TBD-1 of VT-6 prepares to land on USS ENTERPRISE after a raid against Japanese shipping at Kwajalein and Taroa on 1 February 1942. For these missions some of the TBDs carried torpedos while others carried 500 pound bombs on the fuselage bomb racks. (National Archives)

Wing Bomb Racks

Removable Bomb Rack Panels (3 Racks Per Panel)

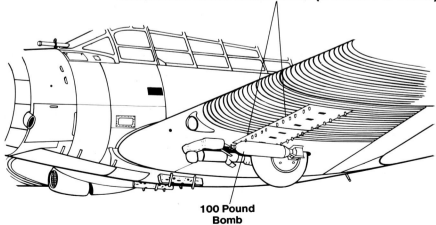

100 Pound
Bomb

Bosn Briggs, a Yellow shirted plane director, signals a TBD-1, with two 500 pound bombs on the centerline racks, to hold while the arresting gear crew clears his hook after landing aboard USS YORKTOWN (CV-5) on 1 February 1942 after the raid on Jaluit Atoll. (Smithsonian Institution)

The Landing Signal Officer aboard ENTERPRISE guides a TBD-1 of VT-6 back aboard after the raid against Kwajalein on 1 February 1942. The aircraft still carries one 500 pound bomb on the port centerline bomb rack. (National Archives)

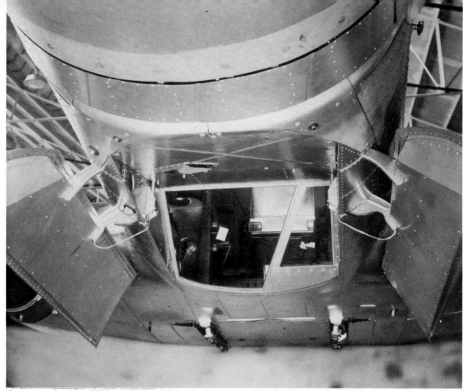

Late production TBD-1s featured redesigned bomb sight doors that were more streamlined than the earlier doors. The door mounts were also altered with the new doors having two supporting arms rather than the three supports used by the earlier style doors. (National Archives)

Center Line Bomb Installation

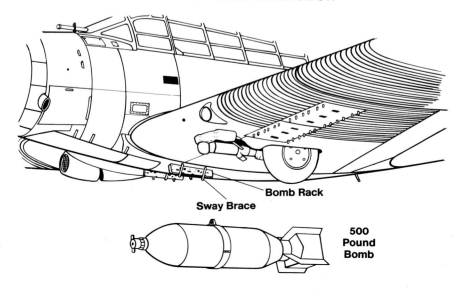

Bomb Rack

Sway Brace

500 Pound Bomb

A TBD-1 of VT-4 takes off from USS RANGER (CV-4) on a scouting mission during early 1942. Originally thought to be too small to operate the TBD, the RANGER took aboard VT-4 during 1941 to give the ship a torpedo bombing capability. The earlier predictions that the ship was too small proved to be wrong. (National Archives)

In March of 1942, USS WASP (CV-7) made a port call at Scapa Flow, Orkney Island, Scotland. Her air group was put ashore and the WASP loaded thirty Spitfires for delivery to Malta. While at Scapa Flow, the TBDs of VT-7 and the F4F Wildcats of VF-71 shared the field with Royal Navy Fairey Fulmar fighters. (National Archives)

The TBDs and SB2Us of USS WASP's Air Group stand by for inspection at Scapa Flow during March of 1942. While at Scapa Flow the TBDs of VT-7 flew anti-submarine patrols over the North Sea and North Atlantic. (National Archives)

TBD-1s of VT-7 spread their wings as they taxi by a DH-89 Rapide at Scapa Flow, Scotland. The TBDs remained at Scapa Flow for three months while USS WASP delivered RAF Spitfires, to Malta. A second trip during April of 1942 led the British Prime Minister, Winston Churchill, to remark, "Who says a WASP can't sting twice?" (National Archives)

Armorers load Blue tipped .30 caliber ammunition into the nose gun of a TBD to ready it for a practice gunnery mission, while other crewmen fuel an F4F Wildcat at Scapa Flow, Scotland during March of 1942. The Blue painted tips of the ammunition left a blue mark on the target, indicating which aircraft hit it. (National Archives)

A TBD-1 makes an arrested landing aboard USS LONG ISLAND (AVG-1) during February of 1942. The LONG ISLAND was a motorship that was converted to a training carrier for Advanced Carrier Training Groups (ACTGs). (National Archives)

Antennas

TBD-1 (Standard)

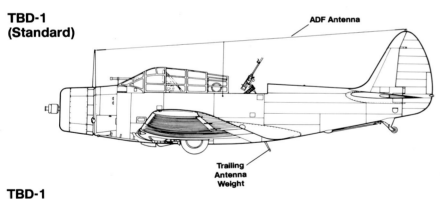

ADF Antenna

Trailing Antenna Weight

TBD-1 (VT-6 Modification)

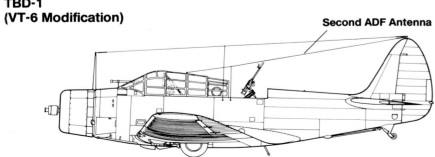

Second ADF Antenna

A TBD-1 of VT-6 makes a practice torpedo drop. VT-6 was one of the first squadrons to repaint their aircraft in the Non-specular Blue Gray over Non-specular Light Gray camouflage authorized in October of 1941. (National Archives)

A TBD-1 deck launches from USS CHARGER (AVG-30) during 1942. The CHARGER operated from Lake Michigan in the training role to train both pilots and deck crews in flight operations in order to provide trained crews for the Fleet. (Smithsonian Institution)

Ground crews position TBDs of VT-8 on the flight line at NAS Norfolk, Virginia during February of 1942. VT-8 received their first TBDs on 3 October 1941 and were assigned to the air group aboard USS HORNET. (National Archives via CAPT W.E. Scarborough)

TBD-1s of VT-8 on the ramp at Naval Air Station, Norfolk, Virginia prior to be being loaded aboard USS HORNET (CV-8) during February of 1942. On departing Norfolk, HORNET steamed to Naval Air Station Alameda, California, off-loaded its TBDs, and loaded Army B-25 bombers for the Doolittle raid on Tokyo. (National Archives)

(Above) A TBD-1 of VT-4 takes off from USS RANGER for a scouting mission in the Atlantic. The RANGER operated out of Guantanamo Bay, Cuba during 1942 flying anti-submarine patrols over the South Atlantic and Caribbean Sea. (National Archives)

(Below) Plane handlers reposition a TBD of VT-4 after a barrier crash aboard USS RANGER during July of 1942. The TBD was not badly damaged and was quickly repaired and back in action flying anti-submarine patrols over the Atlantic.

As their aircrews wait in the cockpits, deck crews make final preparations for launching the TBDs of VT-6 from USS ENTERPRISE for the raid against Wake Island on 24 February 1942. Some of the TBDs still carry the small size national insignia while others have been repainted with a larger star on the fuselage side. (National Archives)

39

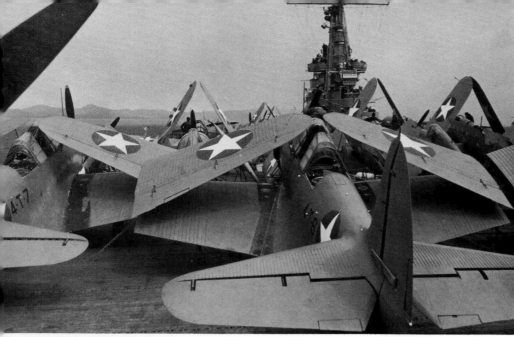

TBDs, SB2Us, and F4Fs crowd the deck of USS RANGER in the South Atlantic during 1942. RANGER would operate the TBD until 27 August 1942, when VT-4 was re-equipped with Grumman TBF Avengers. (National Archives)

The Plane Captain of 6-T-13 turns the inertial starter on this TBD-1 of VT-6 aboard ENTERPRISE during April of 1942. The fold down cowling panel was designed to serve as a work stand for maintenance crews. For scouting missions, the TBDs normally carried a load of 100 pound bombs on the wing racks. (National Archives)

Plane handlers move a TBD-1 on the deck of USS ENTERPRISE prior to the Wake Island raid. The bomb in the foreground is a 500 pound bomb mounted on the port centerline rack of another TBD. The canopy and rudder stripes of the TBD in the background are covered to reduce the possibility that they might be spotted. (National Archives)

A TBD-1 (6-T-5) of VT-6 flies over Wake Island during the ENTERPRISE raid of 24 February 1942. VT-6 would not see action again until the Battle of the Coral Sea some three months later. (Smithsonian Institution)

The Battle of the Coral Sea

As the Japanese racked up victory after victory in the Pacific, the U.S. Navy knew it was just a matter of time before the carrier forces of the two nations faced each other. With only four carriers in the U.S. Pacific fleet, the Navy wanted the time and place to be of their choosing. Unknown to the Japanese, the fleet code had been broken and U.S. intelligence was piecing together the operation plan for their next move, Operation MO, the invasion of Port Moresby. The invasion fleet was to be supported by two Japanese fleet carriers, the *ZUIKAKU* and *SHOKAKU* and the light carrier *SHOHO*.

The Pacific Fleet Commander, ADM Chester W. Nimitz, deployed the carriers LEXINGTON with VT-2 embarked and YORKTOWN with VT-5 aboard to intercept the Japanese invasion force. The plan called for the two carrier task groups, Task Group 17 (YORKTOWN) under RADM Frank J. Fletcher and Task Group 11 (LEXINGTON) under RADM Aubrey Fitch, to join up in the Coral Sea at *Point Buttercup* some 250 miles west of New Hebrides. Here they would form Joint Task Group 17 under the command of RADM Fletcher.

ENTERPRISE under RADM William H. Halsey was returning to Pearl Harbor after escorting HORNET on the Tokyo raid and it would take time to replenish the ship before it could steam westward to reinforce Task Group 17. It was certain that she could not arrive in time to alter the outcome of the coming battle; however, ADM Nimitz decided to accept the risk that the YORKTOWN and LEXINGTON could successfully counter the superior Japanese force without the aid of Halsey's task group.

The opening phase of the battle took place on 3 May 1942 when Japanese troops landed on the island of Tulagi. When he received word of this, RADM Fletcher set course with YORKTOWN to attack the Japanese invasion force. Crews from VT-5 poured over maps of the area in preparation for their attacks against the Japanese warships and transports lying off Tulagi. On 4 May VT-5, along with Douglas SBD dive bombers of VS-5 and Grumman F4F Wildcat fighters of VF-5, they hit the Japanese. One destroyer, a minelayer, a transport and a number of seaplanes were destroyed and the Japanese evacuated the landing force.

On 6 May, YORKTOWN and LEXINGTON joined up and set course to the west to set up an ambush for the approaching Japanese carriers off the Jamard Passage. Unknown to Fletcher, a Japanese floatplane had spotted the two carriers and warned the approaching Japanese fleet. On 7 May, ADM Hara, the Japanese carrier commander, launched search planes to find the American carriers. At 0730 a Japanese scout reported sighting a carrier and a cruiser. Hara immediately ordered out a full strike against this target. Actually, the search aircraft had found the fleet oiler USS NEOSHO and the destroyer USS SIMS.

After searching ahead of the Americans for the carriers they were sure were nearby, the Japanese strike force returned and attacked both ships. The NEOSHO was set afire and the SIMS sunk in less than a minute, after receiving seven hits from Japanese dive bombers. After spending ten days in life rafts, the sixty-eight survivors of the SIMS were finally rescued.

By noon the first of twelve TBDs of VT-2, under LCDR J. H. Brett, were attacking the Japanese light carrier *SHOHO*. None of their torpedos scored a hit, although explosions from near misses blew five Japanese aircraft off the *SHOHO's* deck. As the Devastators finished their runs, SBD Dauntless dive bombers began their attack led by LEXINGTON's air group commander CDR W. B. Ault. As the SBDs dove on the Japanese carrier, ten additional TBDs from VT-5 arrived and began their attacks.

The *SHOHO* turned into the wind to launch its fighters and was a perfect target for the torpedo planes and dive bombers as it steamed a steady course. Bombs hit the flight deck

Deck crews roll modified Bliss-Leavitt Mk XIII torpedos down the deck of USS LEXINGTON. The torpedos were modified with plywood boxes around the propellers to stabilize the torpedo when dropped, and improved firing pins. Unfortunately the modifications did not improve its overall poor performance. (U.S. Navy via Joe Cason)

Bliss-Leavitt Mk XIII Torpedos

Standard Mk XIII

Modified Mk XIII

Plywood Tail Fins

setting it afire forward and several torpedo hits in her boiler room slowed her speed as the carrier lost power. A second group of VT-2 TBDs arrived and now began their runs. Between them, VT-2 and VT-5 scored at least seven torpedo hits and the SBDs added thirteen bomb hits.

Within forty minutes after the attack began, *SHOHO* sank. LCDR R. E. Dixon radioed YORKTOWN, "Scratch one flat top. Dixon to carrier, scratch one flat top." The Japanese navy had lost its first major warship and most of her nine hundred man crew. The attack was a complete success with all but three (two TBDs of VT-5 and one SBD) of the ninety-three aircraft from the American carriers returning safely to base.

In the early morning of 8 May, both forces launched search planes with the same orders, find the carriers. As luck would have it, both sides found each other at almost the same moment. YORKTOWN launched a strike of thirty-nine aircraft, nine TBDs, along with SBDs, escorted by F4Fs against the two Japanese carriers. VT-5, led by LCDR Joe Taylor, began their runs on the *SHOKAKU* at 0915 escorted by Wildcat fighters. Unfortunately, none of the torpedos launched by the TBDs found their mark, all either running wild or failing to explode if they did hit the target. The Japanese also were able to easily evade the slow running Mk XIII torpedos. The SBDs of VB-5 scored several hits and started a fuel fire on *SHOKAKU'S* flight deck. The eleven TBDs of VT-2 had similar problems when they made their attacks and, again, none of the torpedos scored a hit. The attack had cost VT-2 a TBD which ran out of fuel and ditched twenty miles short of the LEXINGTON. The *SHOKAKU* had lost over 100 of her crew; however, the fires were out within an hour and she was able to launch and recover aircraft.

When the strike group arrived back at their carriers they found that the Japanese had found the Task Group. LEXINGTON took two torpedo hits and YORKTOWN had suffered a bomb hit below decks. When the Japanese strike force departed, LEXINGTON

was burning and listing badly. They reported back to their carrier that they had sunk one carrier and severely damaged the second. These reports were somewhat premature. LEXINGTON was able to put out the fires and was now building up speed as the engineers corrected her list. YORKTOWN's single hit had not caused severe damage and she was back in action almost immediately. Both carriers now recovered their strike groups to begin rearming for another strike against the Japanese carriers.

At 1245, LEXINGTON was racked by a huge explosion as fuel vapors below decks were ignited by a stray spark. This set off a chain reaction of explosions as fires raged below decks. As fire crews battled the blaze, LEXINGTON continued making twenty-five knot to recover her strike group. Finally at 1707, ADM Fitch knew that she was doomed and ordered the crew to abandon ship. CAPT Sherman, the ship's commanding officer was the last to leave. LEXINGTON continued to burn as night fell and, at 2200, ADM Fletcher ordered the destroyer USS PHELPS to sink her. When LEXINGTON went down she took all of VT-2s remaining TBDs with her.

The loss of LEXINGTON forced ADM Fletcher to abandon his plans to attack the Japanese carriers and Task Force 17 set course to the southeast for Noumea. Luckily, the Japanese commander believed his pilots' reports and did not pursue the YORKTOWN.

The final tally for the Battle of the Coral Sea was the U.S. one fleet carrier and the Japanese one light carrier. Although a tactical victory for the Japanese, the battle forced the Port Moresby invasion to be called off, resulting in a clear strategic victory for the Americans. Additionally, the myth of Japanese invincibility had been broken, giving the Americans an important psychological victory.

A TBD of VT-5 aboard USS YORKTOWN flies past the splash of a second TBD that was shot down by anti-aircraft gunners aboard the burning Japanese carrier *SHOHO*. (National Archives

(Above) A torpedo explodes on the starboard side of the Imperial Japanese Navy light carrier *SHOHO* during the Battle of the Coral Sea. *SHOHO* was attacked by TBDs of VT-2 (LEXINGTON) and VT-5 (YORKTOWN) besides being bombed by SBDs from both carriers. (National Archives)

(Below) The Japanese carrier *SHOKAKU* was also taken under attack by aircraft of Task Force 17. TBDs from VT-5 attacked the ship first, but their torpedos failed to explode or were out-maneuvered by the carrier. VT-2's later attack produced the same results. Bombs from SBD dive bombers damaged the ship, taking it out of action for some two months. (National Archives)

43

LTJG Preston, Landing Signal Officer aboard USS YORKTOWN (CV-5), gives the cut signal to a TBD of VT-5. During the Battle of the Coral Sea, YORKTOWN was damaged and forced to return to Pearl Harbor for repairs. (Smithsonian Institution)

A fully armed TBD of VT-5 is parked in a revetment in Hawaii during late May of 1942. VT-5 began re-equipping with the TBF Avenger during May and the TBDs were based ashore until they could be returned to California. (National Archives)

USS LEXINGTON (CV-2) was sunk at the Battle of the Coral Sea after she was hit by two torpedos. The hits opened up fuel lines and the explosion of fuel vapors started fires and explosions below decks that doomed the carrier. (National Archives)

MIDWAY

The climatic Battle of Midway would be the end of the TBD's career as a first line torpedo bomber. The Devastator was already scheduled to be replaced by the Grumman TBF Avenger as soon as sufficient quantities of the new Grumman torpedo bomber became available, and VT-8 aboard USS HORNET had already begun conversion training. The squadron had been split, with half remaining at NAS Norfolk, Virginia to begin conversion to the Avenger, while the remainder went to sea aboard USS HORNET, still equipped with the TBD.

Navy Intelligence had warned ADM Nimitz that the next Japanese move would be an invasion of Midway Island. The Japanese planned the attack in the hopes of bringing out the U.S. Pacific Fleet into a decisive battle that the Japanese hoped would decide the Pacific war in their favor. Knowing this, Nimitz planned his own trap for the Japanese fleet, concentrating his remaining forces and positioning his three carriers (YORKTOWN, HORNET, and ENTERPRISE) north of Midway at a point known as *Point Lucky*.

As the squadrons aboard the three carriers prepared for the upcoming battle, the commander of VT-8 ordered that the squadron's TBDs be modified with twin .30 caliber machine guns installed in the rear cockpit. The gun mounts originally had been intended as spares for the SBD squadrons aboard HORNET, but LCDR John Waldron felt that his TBDs would stand a better chance of survival if his gunners had something better than the single .30 caliber machine gun normally carried by the TBD. The other two squadrons, VT-6 on ENTERPRISE and VT-3 on YORKTOWN flew with standard armament.

The opening shots of the battle took place on 4 June 1942 when the Japanese fleet was sighted by a PBY Catalina patrol plane out of Midway. The six TBFs of VT-8's shore based detachment were launched to attack the Japanese along with Army B-17s and Marine SB2Us. In the event, none of the Avengers scored a hit and only one returned to Midway.

At 0700, ENTERPRISE and HORNET launched their strike groups, even though the extreme range meant that the Devastators might not have enough fuel to make it back to their carriers. VT-6 launched fourteen TBDs, while VT-8 launched fifteen. For the pilots of VT-8 the launch was a nervous experience since none had ever taken off from a carrier with a live torpedo; however, they all made it off HORNET safely. The TBDs were the last aircraft off each carrier, and the SBDs were circling for some forty minutes before they were given the signal to proceed to the target without waiting for the slower Devastators. An hour after the SBDs were launched, all the TBDs had finally taken off and were headed toward the Japanese fleet.

The torpedo planes flew at low level toward the enemy, with F4Fs from VF-6 flying as top cover. VT-6 and VF-6 had a prearranged signal that would be used if the TBDs needed help; unfortunately, the TBDs that VF-6 was escorting were those of LCDR John Waldron's VT-8. The Wildcats were flying cover on the wrong squadron, one that did not know the prearranged call for help. At 0930, Waldron sighted the enemy and led his Devastators to attack the *KAGA*. The fifteen TBDs were split into two divisions, eight in one and seven in the second.

Almost immediately, the Devastators were jumped by the Zero fighters of the Japanese combat air patrol. One by one, the TBDs went down under the relentless fighter attacks until just one remained. BuNo 1518, flown by ENS George Gay, was the only VT-8 TBD to actually make a drop on the enemy. Gay was shot down almost immediately after he completed his drop, but he managed to get out of the TBD before it sank. He was the only survivor from Torpedo Eight.

VT-6 followed VT-8 a few minutes later. LCDR Lindsay split his fourteen TBDs into two divisions and maneuvered to set up an anvil attack on *KAGA*. To reach the carrier, the TBDs had to penetrate the outer screen of light cruisers some twelve to fifteen miles out, and an inner screen of heavy cruisers and battleships about six miles out. As the Devastators bored in, the Japanese ships maneuvered to keep VT-6's second division from achieving position to set up an anvil attack. As the TBDs penetrated the outer screen, they were hit by the Zero fighters. By the time the Devastators reached their drop points, only four aircraft remained. While the Devastators were being mauled by the Zeros, VF-6 remained on high cover, waiting for the call that never came. LT Robert Laub successfully made a drop on a Japanese carrier, than broke away and ran for home. As he headed back to the ship his gunner reported seeing explosions on three of the enemy carriers — the SBDs of VB-5 and VB-3 had found the target.

Just prior to the SBD attack, the twelve TBDs of VT-3 along with the seventeen SBDs of VB-3 and six F4Fs of VF-3 arrived over the Japanese fleet. As the TBDs began their runs, they lost contact with VB-3 ending any hopes of a coordinated attack. Led by LCDR Lance Massey, the TBDs were jumped by at least eight Zeros some fifteen miles from the enemy carriers. The enemy fighters made repeated high angle gun passes at the Devastators and, one by one, they were shot down. During the final run in to the target, seven of the twelve TBDs were shot down. Five survived to make drops on the *SORYU*, but the carrier easily evaded the slow Mk XIII torpedos. Three more TBDs were knocked down on their way out, leaving only two to return to ENTERPRISE.

Of the forty-one TBDs launched, only six returned to the Task Force, and one of these ran out of fuel and ditched astern of ENTERPRISE. The casualty rate for the torpedo

Deck handlers position and chock a torpedo armed TBD of VT-6 on the aft aircraft elevator aboard USS ENTERPRISE (CV-6). The wing insignia has been covered over to lessen its visibility from above. (National Archives)

bombers was a staggering ninety percent. The TBD had proven to be too slow to survive in the face of determined fighter attack. Without adequate friendly fighter cover, they were slaughtered.

The sacrifice of the three VT squadrons was not in vain. As the surviving two TBDs of VT-3 made good their escape, chased by the Zero combat air patrol, LCDR Wade McClusky led a total of thirty-seven Dauntless dive bombers from ENTERPRISE down to attack the enemy carriers. These were joined by VB-3 from YORKTOWN. With the Zeros all at low level after dealing with the Devastators, the SBDs had begun their attacks unhindered by enemy fighters.

The SBDs first hit the AKAGI setting fire to the parked aircraft on her flight deck, while a single bomb went through the ships forward elevator exploding among the stowed torpedos on the hangar deck. A few minutes later four bombs hit the KAGA, penetrating the hangar deck and setting her afire as her own bombs and torpedos began going off. VB-3, under LCDR Maxwell E. Leslie, hit the SORYU; again, bombs penetrated the flight deck and exploded among the parked aircraft on the hangar deck, leaving her a burning hulk. ENS Gay, floating in the water, witnessed the destruction of three quarters of the Imperial Japanese Navy's carrier striking force. The cost to the dive bombers was sixteen aircraft from McClusky's group.

The first Japanese counter-attack from the surviving HIRYU damaged the YORKTOWN, but she managed to put out the fires and return to full operation in a short time. The second attack came from six Kate torpedo bombers. Two were shot down but four managed to launch their torpedos from 500 yards out. The damaged YORKTOWN was too slow to evade all the torpedos and two hit her port quarter. As YORKTOWN began to list dramatically, the skipper, CAPT Buckmeister, ordered her abandoned.

While the battle around YORKTOWN raged, her scouting force of ten SBDs that had been launched earlier found the HIRYU. ENTERPRISE immediately launched a force of twenty-four SBDs which arrived over the last Japanese carrier at 1700. Four bombs hit the flight deck in rapid succession, setting her afire. She remained afloat until the next day, a burned out hulk, when she was finally sunk by a Japanese destroyer. For a cost of fifty aircraft and the YORKTOWN, the U.S. Navy had destroyed four fleet carriers, the pride of the Japanese Navy. At midnight on 5 June 1942, ADM Yamamoto sent the signal to the Fleet, "Midway operation is cancelled."

The last action for the TBD was the sinking of the Japanese heavy cruiser MIKUMA on 6 June. The cruiser had been damaged in a collision with the MOGAMI. Their position relayed by an American submarine, ADM Spruance ordered a strike group from ENTERPRISE to attack the two curisers. The three remaining TBDs of VT-6 made up part of the strike group that attacked the MIKUMA and MOGAMI. After the attack by the TBDs and SBDs, the MIKUMA was set afire and sank. The MOGAMI was heavily damaged and eventually reached Truk; however, she would be out of action for almost a year.

Plane handlers move VT-6 TBDs into position on the rear flight deck of USS ENTERPRISE prior to the Battle of Midway. VT-6 would launch a total of fourteen TBDs against the Japanese fleet, recovering only four after the battle. (Smithsonian Institution)

TBDs of Torpedo Squadron Eight (VT-6) are chocked and tied down aboard USS ENTER-PRISE prior to the Battle of Midway. Few of these aircraft would survive the battle and return to their carrier. (National Archives)

The after action reports submitted by YORKTOWN after Midway clearly spelled out the end for the TBD as a first line torpedo bomber. The report conclude that; *It is believed that this engagement clearly shows the vulnerability of the TBD. It is recommended that remaining TBDs be immediately replaced with TBFs.* LT Laub, the ranking surviving officer from all three VT squadrons, submitted his report that stated the Devastators were wiped out because of five main reasons; (1) the skillful maneuvering of the Japanese ships which made the run in to the drop point much longer than anticipated, (2) interception by Zeros, which had ample time to make numerous passes on the TBDs, (3) lack of coordination with the dive bomber squadrons, (4) lack of coordination with the fighter escort, and (5) heavy anti-aircraft fire from the screening ships and the enemy carriers. The TBDs were just too slow to avoid the fighters and flak. He also stated that, although he had flown the TBD for a total of four years, he had never dropped a torpedo in practice until just before the war started.

After Midway, the remaining TBDs in service were quickly withdrawn from front line units. VT-7 was re-equipped with TBFs before USS WASP was transferred to the Pacific. VT-4 aboard USS RANGER retained their TBDs for patrol duty in the Caribbean until August of 1942 when the squadron was decommissioned with the TBDs being transferred to training units ashore.

TBDs were used as trainers at Corpus Christi, Texas until the end of 1942. NAS Maimi operated a number of TBDs until late 1943. Others served at NAS Glenview, Illinois until early 1944 and three were assigned to Dahlgren, Virginia until August of 1944. The last TBD in the inventory was used by the Commander, Fleet Air Activities, West Coast until November of 1944 when it was finally scrapped.

In the six years since the TBD had entered service, it had gone from being the most modern aircraft in the fleet, to being hopelessly outclassed by its opposition. Such was the pace of aircraft development during the critical period just before and during early World War II.

LCDR John C. Waldron was the squadron commander of VT-8 aboard USS HORNET. Prior to the attack on the Japanese at Midway, LCDR Waldron had told his men that even if only one of them survived, he wanted that man to go in and get a hit. (National Archives)

A few days before the Battle of Midway, LCDR John Waldron of VT-8 ordered that the TBDs in the squadron be equipped with twin .30 caliber machine gun mounts. The guns and mounts were taken from the spare parts supplies of the two SBD squadrons aboard USS ENTERPRISE. (U.S. Navy)

A TBD of VT-8 enroute to attack the Japanese fleet at Midway. Of the forty-one TBDs launched by VT-8, VT-6, and VT-3, only six returned to their carriers. None of the torpedo planes scored a hit on the Japanese carriers. (Naval Historical Center)

Rear Gun Position

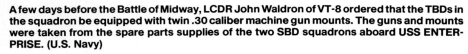

**TBD-1
(Standard)**

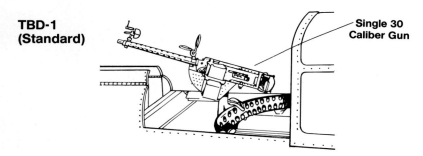

Single 30
Caliber Gun

**TBD-1
(VT-8
Modification)**

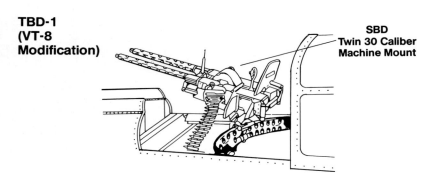

SBD
Twin 30 Caliber
Machine Mount

A TBD of VT-6 just before touchdown on USS ENTERPRISE after the Battle of Midway. VT-6 lost ten of the fourteen TBDs launched against the Japanese fleet. The pace of aircraft development had left the TBD far behind, and by the time of the Battle of Midway it was hopelessly outclassed by Japanese fighters. (National Archives)

Because the Japanese Zero combat air patrol was drawn down to low level to deal with the torpedo attacks of the TBDs, the SBD Dauntless dive bombers were able to attack unopposed by fighters. Thanks to the bravery of the TBD crews, the dive bombers were able to destroy four Japanese carriers. (Walt Holmes)

A survivor of VT-6 lands aboard USS ENTERPRISE after the Battle of Midway. Although greatly outnumbered, the air groups from the three US carriers sank four Japanese carriers and prevented the Japanese fleet from invading Midway. (Naval Historical Center)

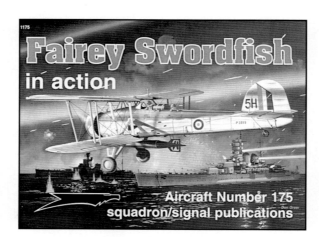